TODAY'S DATE: _____

TODAY I AM FEELING:

☐ 😊 HAPPY
☐ 😐 JUST OKAY
☐ 😞 SAD
☐ 😠 MAD

ONE WORD I WOULD USE TO DESCRIBE TODAY:

_____

ONE THING THAT MADE ME HAPPY TODAY:

_____
_____
_____
_____
_____
_____
_____

ONE THING THAT MADE ME SAD OR MAD TODAY:

_____
_____
_____
_____
_____
_____
_____

ONE THING I LEARNED TODAY:

_____
_____
_____
_____

TODAY'S DATE: _____

TODAY I AM FEELING:

☐ 🙂 HAPPY

☐ 😐 JUST OKAY

☐ 😢 SAD

☐ 😠 MAD

ONE WORD I WOULD USE TO DESCRIBE TODAY:

_____

ONE THING THAT MADE ME HAPPY TODAY:

_____
_____
_____
_____
_____
_____
_____

ONE THING THAT MADE ME SAD OR MAD TODAY:

_____
_____
_____
_____
_____
_____
_____

ONE THING I LEARNED TODAY:

_____
_____
_____
_____

TODAY'S DATE: _____

TODAY I AM FEELING:

- ☐ 😊 HAPPY
- ☐ 😐 JUST OKAY
- ☐ 🙁 SAD
- ☐ 😠 MAD

ONE WORD I WOULD USE TO DESCRIBE TODAY:

_____

ONE THING THAT MADE ME HAPPY TODAY:

_____
_____
_____
_____
_____
_____
_____
_____

ONE THING THAT MADE ME SAD OR MAD TODAY:

_____
_____
_____
_____
_____
_____
_____
_____

ONE THING I LEARNED TODAY:

_____
_____
_____

TODAY'S DATE: _____

TODAY I AM FEELING:

- ☐ 🙂 HAPPY
- ☐ 😐 JUST OKAY
- ☐ ☹️ SAD
- ☐ 😠 MAD

ONE WORD I WOULD USE TO DESCRIBE TODAY:

_____

ONE THING THAT MADE ME HAPPY TODAY:

_____
_____
_____
_____
_____
_____
_____

ONE THING THAT MADE ME SAD OR MAD TODAY:

_____
_____
_____
_____
_____
_____
_____

ONE THING I LEARNED TODAY:

_____
_____
_____

TODAY'S DATE: _____

TODAY I AM FEELING:

- ☐ 😊 HAPPY
- ☐ 😐 JUST OKAY
- ☐ 🙁 SAD
- ☐ 😠 MAD

ONE WORD I WOULD USE TO DESCRIBE TODAY:

ONE THING THAT MADE ME HAPPY TODAY:

ONE THING THAT MADE ME SAD OR MAD TODAY:

ONE THING I LEARNED TODAY:

TODAY'S DATE: _____

TODAY I AM FEELING:

☐ 🙂 HAPPY

☐ 😐 JUST OKAY

☐ ☹️ SAD

☐ 😠 MAD

ONE WORD I WOULD USE TO DESCRIBE TODAY:

_____

ONE THING THAT MADE ME HAPPY TODAY:

_____
_____
_____
_____
_____
_____
_____

ONE THING THAT MADE ME SAD OR MAD TODAY:

_____
_____
_____
_____
_____
_____
_____

ONE THING I LEARNED TODAY:

_____
_____
_____
_____

TODAY'S DATE: _____

TODAY I AM FEELING:

☐ 🙂 HAPPY

☐ 😐 JUST OKAY

☐ 🙁 SAD

☐ 😠 MAD

ONE WORD I WOULD USE TO DESCRIBE TODAY:

_____

ONE THING THAT MADE ME HAPPY TODAY:

_____
_____
_____
_____
_____
_____

ONE THING THAT MADE ME SAD OR MAD TODAY:

_____
_____
_____
_____
_____
_____

ONE THING I LEARNED TODAY:

_____
_____
_____

TODAY'S DATE: _____

TODAY I AM FEELING:

- ☐ 😊 HAPPY
- ☐ 😐 JUST OKAY
- ☐ ☹️ SAD
- ☐ 😠 MAD

ONE WORD I WOULD USE TO DESCRIBE TODAY:

_____

ONE THING THAT MADE ME HAPPY TODAY:

_____
_____
_____
_____
_____
_____
_____

ONE THING THAT MADE ME SAD OR MAD TODAY:

_____
_____
_____
_____
_____
_____
_____

ONE THING I LEARNED TODAY:

_____
_____
_____

TODAY'S DATE: _____

TODAY I AM FEELING:

☐ 🙂 HAPPY

☐ 😐 JUST OKAY

☐ 🙁 SAD

☐ 😠 MAD

ONE WORD I WOULD USE TO DESCRIBE TODAY:

_____

ONE THING THAT MADE ME HAPPY TODAY:

_____
_____
_____
_____
_____
_____
_____

ONE THING THAT MADE ME SAD OR MAD TODAY:

_____
_____
_____
_____
_____
_____
_____

ONE THING I LEARNED TODAY:

_____
_____
_____

TODAY'S DATE: _____

TODAY I AM FEELING:

☐ 🙂 HAPPY

☐ 😐 JUST OKAY

☐ 🙁 SAD

☐ ☹️ MAD

ONE WORD I WOULD USE TO DESCRIBE TODAY:

ONE THING THAT MADE ME HAPPY TODAY:

ONE THING THAT MADE ME SAD OR MAD TODAY:

ONE THING I LEARNED TODAY:

TODAY'S DATE: _____

TODAY I AM FEELING:

- [ ] 🙂 HAPPY
- [ ] 😐 JUST OKAY
- [ ] ☹️ SAD
- [ ] 😠 MAD

ONE WORD I WOULD USE TO DESCRIBE TODAY:

_____

ONE THING THAT MADE ME HAPPY TODAY:

_____
_____
_____
_____
_____
_____
_____

ONE THING THAT MADE ME SAD OR MAD TODAY:

_____
_____
_____
_____
_____
_____
_____

ONE THING I LEARNED TODAY:

_____
_____
_____
_____

TODAY'S DATE: _____

TODAY I AM FEELING:

☐ 😊 HAPPY

☐ 😐 JUST OKAY

☐ 😟 SAD

☐ 😠 MAD

ONE WORD I WOULD USE TO DESCRIBE TODAY:

_____

ONE THING THAT MADE ME HAPPY TODAY:

_____
_____
_____
_____
_____
_____
_____

ONE THING THAT MADE ME SAD OR MAD TODAY:

_____
_____
_____
_____
_____
_____
_____

ONE THING I LEARNED TODAY:

_____
_____
_____

TODAY'S DATE: _____

TODAY I AM FEELING:

☐ 😊 HAPPY

☐ 😐 JUST OKAY

☐ 🙁 SAD

☐ 😠 MAD

ONE WORD I WOULD USE TO DESCRIBE TODAY:

ONE THING THAT MADE ME HAPPY TODAY:

ONE THING THAT MADE ME SAD OR MAD TODAY:

ONE THING I LEARNED TODAY:

TODAY'S DATE: _____

TODAY I AM FEELING:

☐ 🙂 HAPPY

☐ 😐 JUST OKAY

☐ ☹️ SAD

☐ 😠 MAD

ONE WORD I WOULD USE TO DESCRIBE TODAY:

_____

ONE THING THAT MADE ME HAPPY TODAY:

_____
_____
_____
_____
_____
_____
_____

ONE THING THAT MADE ME SAD OR MAD TODAY:

_____
_____
_____
_____
_____
_____
_____

ONE THING I LEARNED TODAY:

_____
_____
_____

TODAY'S DATE: _____

TODAY I AM FEELING:

- ☐ 😊 HAPPY
- ☐ 😐 JUST OKAY
- ☐ 🙁 SAD
- ☐ 😠 MAD

ONE WORD I WOULD USE TO DESCRIBE TODAY:

_____

ONE THING THAT MADE ME HAPPY TODAY:

_____
_____
_____
_____
_____
_____
_____

ONE THING THAT MADE ME SAD OR MAD TODAY:

_____
_____
_____
_____
_____
_____
_____

ONE THING I LEARNED TODAY:

_____
_____
_____
_____

TODAY'S DATE: _____

TODAY I AM FEELING:

- ☐ 🙂 HAPPY
- ☐ 😐 JUST OKAY
- ☐ 🙁 SAD
- ☐ 😠 MAD

ONE WORD I WOULD USE TO DESCRIBE TODAY:

_____

ONE THING THAT MADE ME HAPPY TODAY:

_____
_____
_____
_____
_____
_____
_____
_____

ONE THING THAT MADE ME SAD OR MAD TODAY:

_____
_____
_____
_____
_____
_____
_____
_____

ONE THING I LEARNED TODAY:

_____
_____
_____
_____

TODAY'S DATE: _____

TODAY I AM FEELING:

- ☐ 🙂 HAPPY
- ☐ 😐 JUST OKAY
- ☐ 🙁 SAD
- ☐ 😠 MAD

ONE WORD I WOULD USE TO DESCRIBE TODAY:

_____

ONE THING THAT MADE ME HAPPY TODAY:

_____
_____
_____
_____
_____
_____
_____

ONE THING THAT MADE ME SAD OR MAD TODAY:

_____
_____
_____
_____
_____
_____
_____

ONE THING I LEARNED TODAY:

_____
_____
_____

TODAY'S DATE: _____

TODAY I AM FEELING:

- ☐ 🙂 HAPPY
- ☐ 😐 JUST OKAY
- ☐ 🙁 SAD
- ☐ 😠 MAD

ONE WORD I WOULD USE TO DESCRIBE TODAY:

_____

ONE THING THAT MADE ME HAPPY TODAY:

_____
_____
_____
_____
_____
_____
_____

ONE THING THAT MADE ME SAD OR MAD TODAY:

_____
_____
_____
_____
_____
_____
_____

ONE THING I LEARNED TODAY:

_____
_____
_____

TODAY'S DATE: _____

TODAY I AM FEELING:

- [ ] 🙂 HAPPY
- [ ] 😐 JUST OKAY
- [ ] 🙁 SAD
- [ ] 😠 MAD

ONE WORD I WOULD USE TO DESCRIBE TODAY:

_____

ONE THING THAT MADE ME HAPPY TODAY:

_____
_____
_____
_____
_____
_____
_____

ONE THING THAT MADE ME SAD OR MAD TODAY:

_____
_____
_____
_____
_____
_____
_____

ONE THING I LEARNED TODAY:

_____
_____
_____
_____

TODAY'S DATE: _____

TODAY I AM FEELING:

☐ 😊 HAPPY
☐ 😐 JUST OKAY
☐ 😟 SAD
☐ 😠 MAD

ONE WORD I WOULD USE TO DESCRIBE TODAY:

_____

ONE THING THAT MADE ME HAPPY TODAY:

_____
_____
_____
_____
_____
_____
_____

ONE THING THAT MADE ME SAD OR MAD TODAY:

_____
_____
_____
_____
_____
_____
_____

ONE THING I LEARNED TODAY:

_____
_____
_____
_____

TODAY'S DATE: _____

TODAY I AM FEELING:

- ☐ 😊 HAPPY
- ☐ 😐 JUST OKAY
- ☐ 😟 SAD
- ☐ 😠 MAD

ONE WORD I WOULD USE TO DESCRIBE TODAY:

_____

ONE THING THAT MADE ME HAPPY TODAY:

_____
_____
_____
_____
_____
_____

ONE THING THAT MADE ME SAD OR MAD TODAY:

_____
_____
_____
_____
_____
_____

ONE THING I LEARNED TODAY:

_____
_____
_____
_____

TODAY'S DATE: _____

TODAY I AM FEELING:

- ☐ 🙂 HAPPY
- ☐ 😐 JUST OKAY
- ☐ ☹️ SAD
- ☐ 😠 MAD

ONE WORD I WOULD USE TO DESCRIBE TODAY:

_____

ONE THING THAT MADE ME HAPPY TODAY:

_____
_____
_____
_____
_____
_____
_____

ONE THING THAT MADE ME SAD OR MAD TODAY:

_____
_____
_____
_____
_____
_____
_____

ONE THING I LEARNED TODAY:

_____
_____
_____

TODAY'S DATE: _____

TODAY I AM FEELING:

☐ 😊 HAPPY

☐ 😐 JUST OKAY

☐ 🙁 SAD

☐ 😠 MAD

ONE WORD I WOULD USE TO DESCRIBE TODAY:

_____

ONE THING THAT MADE ME HAPPY TODAY:

_____
_____
_____
_____
_____
_____
_____

ONE THING THAT MADE ME SAD OR MAD TODAY:

_____
_____
_____
_____
_____
_____
_____

ONE THING I LEARNED TODAY:

_____
_____
_____

TODAY'S DATE: _____

TODAY I AM FEELING:

- ☐ 🙂 HAPPY
- ☐ 😐 JUST OKAY
- ☐ 🙁 SAD
- ☐ 😠 MAD

ONE WORD I WOULD USE TO DESCRIBE TODAY:

_____

ONE THING THAT MADE ME HAPPY TODAY:

_____
_____
_____
_____
_____
_____
_____

ONE THING THAT MADE ME SAD OR MAD TODAY:

_____
_____
_____
_____
_____
_____
_____

ONE THING I LEARNED TODAY:

_____
_____
_____

TODAY'S DATE: _____

TODAY I AM FEELING:

- ☐ 😊 HAPPY
- ☐ 😐 JUST OKAY
- ☐ 🙁 SAD
- ☐ 😠 MAD

ONE WORD I WOULD USE TO DESCRIBE TODAY:

_____

ONE THING THAT MADE ME HAPPY TODAY:

_____
_____
_____
_____
_____
_____

ONE THING THAT MADE ME SAD OR MAD TODAY:

_____
_____
_____
_____
_____
_____

ONE THING I LEARNED TODAY:

_____
_____
_____

TODAY'S DATE: _____

TODAY I AM FEELING:

☐ 🙂 HAPPY
☐ 😐 JUST OKAY
☐ 🙁 SAD
☐ 😠 MAD

ONE WORD I WOULD USE TO DESCRIBE TODAY:

_____

ONE THING THAT MADE ME HAPPY TODAY:

_____
_____
_____
_____
_____
_____
_____

ONE THING THAT MADE ME SAD OR MAD TODAY:

_____
_____
_____
_____
_____
_____
_____

ONE THING I LEARNED TODAY:

_____
_____
_____

TODAY'S DATE: _____

TODAY I AM FEELING:

☐ 😊 HAPPY

☐ 😐 JUST OKAY

☐ 😢 SAD

☐ 😠 MAD

ONE WORD I WOULD USE TO DESCRIBE TODAY:

_____

ONE THING THAT MADE ME HAPPY TODAY:

_____
_____
_____
_____
_____
_____

ONE THING THAT MADE ME SAD OR MAD TODAY:

_____
_____
_____
_____
_____
_____

ONE THING I LEARNED TODAY:

_____
_____
_____

TODAY'S DATE: _____

TODAY I AM FEELING:

- [ ] 🙂 HAPPY
- [ ] 😐 JUST OKAY
- [ ] ☹️ SAD
- [ ] 😠 MAD

ONE WORD I WOULD USE TO DESCRIBE TODAY:

_____

ONE THING THAT MADE ME HAPPY TODAY:

_____
_____
_____
_____
_____
_____
_____

ONE THING THAT MADE ME SAD OR MAD TODAY:

_____
_____
_____
_____
_____
_____
_____

ONE THING I LEARNED TODAY:

_____
_____
_____

TODAY'S DATE: _____

TODAY I AM FEELING:

- ☐ 🙂 HAPPY
- ☐ 😐 JUST OKAY
- ☐ 🙁 SAD
- ☐ ☹️ MAD

ONE WORD I WOULD USE TO DESCRIBE TODAY:

_____

ONE THING THAT MADE ME HAPPY TODAY:

_____
_____
_____
_____
_____
_____

ONE THING THAT MADE ME SAD OR MAD TODAY:

_____
_____
_____
_____
_____
_____

ONE THING I LEARNED TODAY:

_____
_____
_____

TODAY'S DATE: _____

TODAY I AM FEELING:

☐ 🙂 HAPPY

☐ 😐 JUST OKAY

☐ 🙁 SAD

☐ 😠 MAD

ONE WORD I WOULD USE TO
DESCRIBE TODAY:

_____

ONE THING THAT MADE
ME HAPPY TODAY:

_____
_____
_____
_____
_____
_____
_____

ONE THING THAT MADE
ME SAD OR MAD TODAY:

_____
_____
_____
_____
_____
_____
_____

ONE THING I LEARNED TODAY:

_____
_____
_____
_____

TODAY'S DATE: _____

TODAY I AM FEELING:

- ☐ 🙂 HAPPY
- ☐ 😐 JUST OKAY
- ☐ 🙁 SAD
- ☐ 😠 MAD

ONE WORD I WOULD USE TO DESCRIBE TODAY:

_____

ONE THING THAT MADE ME HAPPY TODAY:

_____
_____
_____
_____
_____

ONE THING THAT MADE ME SAD OR MAD TODAY:

_____
_____
_____
_____
_____

ONE THING I LEARNED TODAY:

_____
_____
_____
_____

TODAY'S DATE: _____

TODAY I AM FEELING:

- [ ] 😊 HAPPY
- [ ] 😐 JUST OKAY
- [ ] 😞 SAD
- [ ] 😠 MAD

ONE WORD I WOULD USE TO DESCRIBE TODAY:

_____

ONE THING THAT MADE ME HAPPY TODAY:

_____
_____
_____
_____
_____
_____
_____

ONE THING THAT MADE ME SAD OR MAD TODAY:

_____
_____
_____
_____
_____
_____
_____

ONE THING I LEARNED TODAY:

_____
_____
_____
_____

TODAY'S DATE: _____

TODAY I AM FEELING:

- ☐ 🙂 HAPPY
- ☐ 😐 JUST OKAY
- ☐ 🙁 SAD
- ☐ 😠 MAD

ONE WORD I WOULD USE TO DESCRIBE TODAY:

_____

ONE THING THAT MADE ME HAPPY TODAY:

_____
_____
_____
_____
_____
_____

ONE THING THAT MADE ME SAD OR MAD TODAY:

_____
_____
_____
_____
_____
_____

ONE THING I LEARNED TODAY:

_____
_____
_____
_____

TODAY'S DATE: _____

TODAY I AM FEELING:

- ☐ 😊 HAPPY
- ☐ 😐 JUST OKAY
- ☐ ☹️ SAD
- ☐ 😠 MAD

ONE WORD I WOULD USE TO DESCRIBE TODAY:

_____

ONE THING THAT MADE ME HAPPY TODAY:

_____
_____
_____
_____
_____
_____
_____

ONE THING THAT MADE ME SAD OR MAD TODAY:

_____
_____
_____
_____
_____
_____

ONE THING I LEARNED TODAY:

_____
_____
_____

TODAY'S DATE: _____

TODAY I AM FEELING:

- [ ] 🙂 HAPPY
- [ ] 😐 JUST OKAY
- [ ] 🙁 SAD
- [ ] 😠 MAD

ONE WORD I WOULD USE TO DESCRIBE TODAY:

_____

ONE THING THAT MADE ME HAPPY TODAY:

_____
_____
_____
_____
_____
_____
_____

ONE THING THAT MADE ME SAD OR MAD TODAY:

_____
_____
_____
_____
_____
_____
_____

ONE THING I LEARNED TODAY:

_____
_____
_____
_____

TODAY'S DATE: _____

TODAY I AM FEELING:

☐ 🙂 HAPPY

☐ 😐 JUST OKAY

☐ 🙁 SAD

☐ 😠 MAD

ONE WORD I WOULD USE TO DESCRIBE TODAY:

_____

ONE THING THAT MADE ME HAPPY TODAY:

_____
_____
_____
_____
_____
_____
_____
_____

ONE THING THAT MADE ME SAD OR MAD TODAY:

_____
_____
_____
_____
_____
_____
_____
_____

ONE THING I LEARNED TODAY:

_____
_____
_____
_____

TODAY'S DATE: _____

TODAY I AM FEELING:

- ☐ ☺ HAPPY
- ☐ 😐 JUST OKAY
- ☐ ☹ SAD
- ☐ 😠 MAD

ONE WORD I WOULD USE TO DESCRIBE TODAY:

_____

ONE THING THAT MADE ME HAPPY TODAY:

_____
_____
_____
_____
_____
_____
_____

ONE THING THAT MADE ME SAD OR MAD TODAY:

_____
_____
_____
_____
_____
_____
_____

ONE THING I LEARNED TODAY:

_____
_____
_____
_____

TODAY'S DATE: _____

TODAY I AM FEELING:

☐ 🙂 HAPPY
☐ 😐 JUST OKAY
☐ 🙁 SAD
☐ 😠 MAD

ONE WORD I WOULD USE TO DESCRIBE TODAY:
_____

ONE THING THAT MADE ME HAPPY TODAY:
_____
_____
_____
_____
_____
_____
_____

ONE THING THAT MADE ME SAD OR MAD TODAY:
_____
_____
_____
_____
_____
_____
_____

ONE THING I LEARNED TODAY:
_____
_____
_____

TODAY'S DATE: _____

TODAY I AM FEELING:

☐ 😊 HAPPY

☐ 😐 JUST OKAY

☐ 😟 SAD

☐ 😠 MAD

ONE WORD I WOULD USE TO DESCRIBE TODAY:

_____

ONE THING THAT MADE ME HAPPY TODAY:

_____
_____
_____
_____
_____
_____

ONE THING THAT MADE ME SAD OR MAD TODAY:

_____
_____
_____
_____
_____

ONE THING I LEARNED TODAY:

_____
_____
_____

TODAY'S DATE: _____

TODAY I AM FEELING:

☐ 😊 HAPPY

☐ 😐 JUST OKAY

☐ 😞 SAD

☐ 😠 MAD

ONE WORD I WOULD USE TO DESCRIBE TODAY:

_____

ONE THING THAT MADE ME HAPPY TODAY:

_____
_____
_____
_____
_____
_____
_____

ONE THING THAT MADE ME SAD OR MAD TODAY:

_____
_____
_____
_____
_____
_____
_____

ONE THING I LEARNED TODAY:

_____
_____
_____

TODAY'S DATE: _____

TODAY I AM FEELING:

- [ ] 😊 HAPPY
- [ ] 😐 JUST OKAY
- [ ] 🙁 SAD
- [ ] 😠 MAD

ONE WORD I WOULD USE TO DESCRIBE TODAY:

_____

ONE THING THAT MADE ME HAPPY TODAY:

_____
_____
_____
_____
_____
_____

ONE THING THAT MADE ME SAD OR MAD TODAY:

_____
_____
_____
_____
_____
_____

ONE THING I LEARNED TODAY:

_____
_____
_____
_____

TODAY'S DATE: _____

TODAY I AM FEELING:

☐ 😊 HAPPY
☐ 😐 JUST OKAY
☐ 😢 SAD
☐ 😠 MAD

ONE WORD I WOULD USE TO
DESCRIBE TODAY:

_____

ONE THING THAT MADE
ME HAPPY TODAY:

_____
_____
_____
_____
_____
_____
_____

ONE THING THAT MADE
ME SAD OR MAD TODAY:

_____
_____
_____
_____
_____
_____
_____

ONE THING I LEARNED TODAY:

_____
_____
_____

TODAY'S DATE: _____

TODAY I AM FEELING:

☐ 🙂 HAPPY
☐ 😐 JUST OKAY
☐ 🙁 SAD
☐ 😠 MAD

ONE WORD I WOULD USE TO DESCRIBE TODAY:

_____

ONE THING THAT MADE ME HAPPY TODAY:

_____
_____
_____
_____
_____
_____

ONE THING THAT MADE ME SAD OR MAD TODAY:

_____
_____
_____
_____
_____
_____

ONE THING I LEARNED TODAY:

_____
_____
_____

TODAY'S DATE: _____

TODAY I AM FEELING:

☐ 🙂 HAPPY

☐ 😐 JUST OKAY

☐ 🙁 SAD

☐ 😠 MAD

ONE WORD I WOULD USE TO DESCRIBE TODAY:

_____

ONE THING THAT MADE ME HAPPY TODAY:

_____
_____
_____
_____
_____
_____
_____

ONE THING THAT MADE ME SAD OR MAD TODAY:

_____
_____
_____
_____
_____
_____

ONE THING I LEARNED TODAY:

_____
_____
_____
_____

TODAY'S DATE: _____

TODAY I AM FEELING:

- [ ] 😊 HAPPY
- [ ] 😐 JUST OKAY
- [ ] 🙁 SAD
- [ ] 😠 MAD

ONE WORD I WOULD USE TO DESCRIBE TODAY:

_____

ONE THING THAT MADE ME HAPPY TODAY:

_____
_____
_____
_____
_____
_____

ONE THING THAT MADE ME SAD OR MAD TODAY:

_____
_____
_____
_____
_____
_____

ONE THING I LEARNED TODAY:

_____
_____
_____
_____

TODAY'S DATE: _____

TODAY I AM FEELING:

☐ 😊 HAPPY

☐ 😐 JUST OKAY

☐ 😞 SAD

☐ 😠 MAD

ONE WORD I WOULD USE TO DESCRIBE TODAY:

_____

ONE THING THAT MADE ME HAPPY TODAY:

_____
_____
_____
_____
_____
_____
_____
_____

ONE THING THAT MADE ME SAD OR MAD TODAY:

_____
_____
_____
_____
_____
_____
_____
_____

ONE THING I LEARNED TODAY:

_____
_____
_____
_____

TODAY'S DATE: _____

TODAY I AM FEELING:

☐ 😊 HAPPY

☐ 😐 JUST OKAY

☐ 😟 SAD

☐ 😠 MAD

ONE WORD I WOULD USE TO DESCRIBE TODAY:

_____

ONE THING THAT MADE ME HAPPY TODAY:

_____
_____
_____
_____
_____
_____

ONE THING THAT MADE ME SAD OR MAD TODAY:

_____
_____
_____
_____
_____
_____

ONE THING I LEARNED TODAY:

_____
_____
_____

TODAY'S DATE: _____

TODAY I AM FEELING:

- ☐ 🙂 HAPPY
- ☐ 😐 JUST OKAY
- ☐ ☹️ SAD
- ☐ 😠 MAD

ONE WORD I WOULD USE TO DESCRIBE TODAY:
_____

ONE THING THAT MADE ME HAPPY TODAY:
_____
_____
_____
_____
_____
_____
_____

ONE THING THAT MADE ME SAD OR MAD TODAY:
_____
_____
_____
_____
_____
_____
_____

ONE THING I LEARNED TODAY:
_____
_____
_____

TODAY'S DATE: _____

TODAY I AM FEELING:

- ☐ 🙂 HAPPY
- ☐ 😐 JUST OKAY
- ☐ ☹️ SAD
- ☐ 😠 MAD

ONE WORD I WOULD USE TO DESCRIBE TODAY:

_____

ONE THING THAT MADE ME HAPPY TODAY:

_____
_____
_____
_____
_____
_____

ONE THING THAT MADE ME SAD OR MAD TODAY:

_____
_____
_____
_____
_____
_____

ONE THING I LEARNED TODAY:

_____
_____
_____

TODAY'S DATE: _____

TODAY I AM FEELING:

- ☐ 🙂 HAPPY
- ☐ 😐 JUST OKAY
- ☐ 🙁 SAD
- ☐ 😠 MAD

ONE WORD I WOULD USE TO DESCRIBE TODAY:

ONE THING THAT MADE ME HAPPY TODAY:

ONE THING THAT MADE ME SAD OR MAD TODAY:

ONE THING I LEARNED TODAY:

TODAY'S DATE: _____

TODAY I AM FEELING:

☐ 🙂 HAPPY
☐ 😐 JUST OKAY
☐ 🙁 SAD
☐ 😠 MAD

ONE WORD I WOULD USE TO DESCRIBE TODAY:

_____

ONE THING THAT MADE ME HAPPY TODAY:

_____
_____
_____
_____
_____
_____

ONE THING THAT MADE ME SAD OR MAD TODAY:

_____
_____
_____
_____
_____
_____

ONE THING I LEARNED TODAY:

_____
_____
_____
_____

TODAY'S DATE: _____

TODAY I AM FEELING:

☐ 😊 HAPPY
☐ 😐 JUST OKAY
☐ 😞 SAD
☐ 😠 MAD

ONE WORD I WOULD USE TO DESCRIBE TODAY:

_____

ONE THING THAT MADE ME HAPPY TODAY:

_____
_____
_____
_____
_____
_____
_____
_____

ONE THING THAT MADE ME SAD OR MAD TODAY:

_____
_____
_____
_____
_____
_____
_____
_____

ONE THING I LEARNED TODAY:

_____
_____
_____

TODAY'S DATE: _____

TODAY I AM FEELING:

- [ ] 😊 HAPPY
- [ ] 😐 JUST OKAY
- [ ] 😢 SAD
- [ ] 😠 MAD

ONE WORD I WOULD USE TO DESCRIBE TODAY:

_____

ONE THING THAT MADE ME HAPPY TODAY:

_____
_____
_____
_____
_____
_____

ONE THING THAT MADE ME SAD OR MAD TODAY:

_____
_____
_____
_____
_____
_____

ONE THING I LEARNED TODAY:

_____
_____
_____

TODAY'S DATE: _____

TODAY I AM FEELING:

☐ 😊 HAPPY

☐ 😐 JUST OKAY

☐ 😞 SAD

☐ 😠 MAD

ONE WORD I WOULD USE TO DESCRIBE TODAY:

_____

ONE THING THAT MADE ME HAPPY TODAY:

_____
_____
_____
_____
_____
_____

ONE THING THAT MADE ME SAD OR MAD TODAY:

_____
_____
_____
_____
_____
_____

ONE THING I LEARNED TODAY:

_____
_____
_____

TODAY'S DATE: _____

TODAY I AM FEELING:

- [ ] 😊 HAPPY
- [ ] 😐 JUST OKAY
- [ ] 😢 SAD
- [ ] 😠 MAD

ONE WORD I WOULD USE TO DESCRIBE TODAY:

_____

ONE THING THAT MADE ME HAPPY TODAY:

_____
_____
_____
_____
_____
_____
_____

ONE THING THAT MADE ME SAD OR MAD TODAY:

_____
_____
_____
_____
_____
_____
_____

ONE THING I LEARNED TODAY:

_____
_____
_____
_____

TODAY'S DATE: _____

TODAY I AM FEELING:

☐ 🙂 HAPPY

☐ 😐 JUST OKAY

☐ 🙁 SAD

☐ 😠 MAD

ONE WORD I WOULD USE TO DESCRIBE TODAY:

_____

ONE THING THAT MADE ME HAPPY TODAY:

_____
_____
_____
_____
_____
_____
_____

ONE THING THAT MADE ME SAD OR MAD TODAY:

_____
_____
_____
_____
_____
_____

ONE THING I LEARNED TODAY:

_____
_____
_____

TODAY'S DATE: _____

TODAY I AM FEELING:

☐ 🙂 HAPPY
☐ 😐 JUST OKAY
☐ ☹️ SAD
☐ 😠 MAD

ONE WORD I WOULD USE TO DESCRIBE TODAY:

_____

ONE THING THAT MADE ME HAPPY TODAY:

_____
_____
_____
_____
_____
_____

ONE THING THAT MADE ME SAD OR MAD TODAY:

_____
_____
_____
_____
_____
_____

ONE THING I LEARNED TODAY:

_____
_____
_____
_____

TODAY'S DATE: _____

TODAY I AM FEELING:

☐ ☺ HAPPY

☐ 😐 JUST OKAY

☐ ☹ SAD

☐ 😠 MAD

ONE WORD I WOULD USE TO DESCRIBE TODAY:

_____

ONE THING THAT MADE ME HAPPY TODAY:

_____
_____
_____
_____
_____
_____
_____
_____

ONE THING THAT MADE ME SAD OR MAD TODAY:

_____
_____
_____
_____
_____
_____
_____
_____

ONE THING I LEARNED TODAY:

_____
_____
_____

TODAY'S DATE: _____

TODAY I AM FEELING:

- ☐ 😊 HAPPY
- ☐ 😐 JUST OKAY
- ☐ 😞 SAD
- ☐ 😠 MAD

ONE WORD I WOULD USE TO DESCRIBE TODAY:

_____

ONE THING THAT MADE ME HAPPY TODAY:

_____
_____
_____
_____
_____
_____
_____

ONE THING THAT MADE ME SAD OR MAD TODAY:

_____
_____
_____
_____
_____
_____
_____

ONE THING I LEARNED TODAY:

_____
_____
_____
_____

TODAY'S DATE: _____

TODAY I AM FEELING:

- ☐ 😊 HAPPY
- ☐ 😐 JUST OKAY
- ☐ 🙁 SAD
- ☐ 😠 MAD

ONE WORD I WOULD USE TO DESCRIBE TODAY:

_____

ONE THING THAT MADE ME HAPPY TODAY:

_____
_____
_____
_____
_____
_____
_____

ONE THING THAT MADE ME SAD OR MAD TODAY:

_____
_____
_____
_____
_____

ONE THING I LEARNED TODAY:

_____
_____
_____

TODAY'S DATE: _____

TODAY I AM FEELING:

- [ ] 😊 HAPPY
- [ ] 😐 JUST OKAY
- [ ] 😞 SAD
- [ ] 😠 MAD

ONE WORD I WOULD USE TO DESCRIBE TODAY:

_____

ONE THING THAT MADE ME HAPPY TODAY:

_____
_____
_____
_____
_____
_____

ONE THING THAT MADE ME SAD OR MAD TODAY:

_____
_____
_____
_____
_____
_____

ONE THING I LEARNED TODAY:

_____
_____
_____

TODAY'S DATE: _____

TODAY I AM FEELING:

☐ 🙂 HAPPY

☐ 😐 JUST OKAY

☐ 🙁 SAD

☐ 😠 MAD

ONE WORD I WOULD USE TO DESCRIBE TODAY:

_____

ONE THING THAT MADE ME HAPPY TODAY:

_____
_____
_____
_____
_____
_____
_____

ONE THING THAT MADE ME SAD OR MAD TODAY:

_____
_____
_____
_____
_____
_____
_____

ONE THING I LEARNED TODAY:

_____
_____
_____

TODAY'S DATE: _____

TODAY I AM FEELING:

- ☐ 😊 HAPPY
- ☐ 😐 JUST OKAY
- ☐ 😞 SAD
- ☐ 😠 MAD

ONE WORD I WOULD USE TO DESCRIBE TODAY:

_____

ONE THING THAT MADE ME HAPPY TODAY:

_____
_____
_____
_____
_____
_____
_____

ONE THING THAT MADE ME SAD OR MAD TODAY:

_____
_____
_____
_____
_____
_____
_____

ONE THING I LEARNED TODAY:

_____
_____
_____
_____

TODAY'S DATE: _____

TODAY I AM FEELING:

- ☐ 🙂 HAPPY
- ☐ 😐 JUST OKAY
- ☐ 🙁 SAD
- ☐ 😠 MAD

ONE WORD I WOULD USE TO DESCRIBE TODAY:

_____

ONE THING THAT MADE ME HAPPY TODAY:

_____
_____
_____
_____
_____
_____

ONE THING THAT MADE ME SAD OR MAD TODAY:

_____
_____
_____
_____
_____
_____

ONE THING I LEARNED TODAY:

_____
_____
_____

TODAY'S DATE: _____

TODAY I AM FEELING:

☐ 😊 HAPPY
☐ 😐 JUST OKAY
☐ 😟 SAD
☐ 😠 MAD

ONE WORD I WOULD USE TO DESCRIBE TODAY:

_____

ONE THING THAT MADE ME HAPPY TODAY:

_____
_____
_____
_____
_____
_____

ONE THING THAT MADE ME SAD OR MAD TODAY:

_____
_____
_____
_____
_____
_____

ONE THING I LEARNED TODAY:

_____
_____
_____

TODAY'S DATE: _____

TODAY I AM FEELING:

☐ 🙂 HAPPY

☐ 😐 JUST OKAY

☐ 🙁 SAD

☐ 😠 MAD

ONE WORD I WOULD USE TO DESCRIBE TODAY:

_____

ONE THING THAT MADE ME HAPPY TODAY:

_____
_____
_____
_____
_____
_____
_____
_____

ONE THING THAT MADE ME SAD OR MAD TODAY:

_____
_____
_____
_____
_____
_____
_____
_____

ONE THING I LEARNED TODAY:

_____
_____
_____

TODAY'S DATE: _____

TODAY I AM FEELING:

- ☐ 😊 HAPPY
- ☐ 😐 JUST OKAY
- ☐ 😞 SAD
- ☐ 😠 MAD

ONE WORD I WOULD USE TO DESCRIBE TODAY:

_____

ONE THING THAT MADE ME HAPPY TODAY:

_____
_____
_____
_____
_____
_____
_____

ONE THING THAT MADE ME SAD OR MAD TODAY:

_____
_____
_____
_____
_____
_____
_____

ONE THING I LEARNED TODAY:

_____
_____
_____

TODAY'S DATE: _____

TODAY I AM FEELING:

- [ ] 😊 HAPPY
- [ ] 😐 JUST OKAY
- [ ] ☹️ SAD
- [ ] 😠 MAD

ONE WORD I WOULD USE TO DESCRIBE TODAY:

_____

ONE THING THAT MADE ME HAPPY TODAY:

_____
_____
_____
_____
_____
_____
_____

ONE THING THAT MADE ME SAD OR MAD TODAY:

_____
_____
_____
_____
_____
_____
_____

ONE THING I LEARNED TODAY:

_____
_____
_____

TODAY'S DATE: _____

TODAY I AM FEELING:

☐ 😊 HAPPY
☐ 😐 JUST OKAY
☐ 🙁 SAD
☐ 😠 MAD

ONE WORD I WOULD USE TO DESCRIBE TODAY:

_____

ONE THING THAT MADE ME HAPPY TODAY:

_____
_____
_____
_____
_____
_____

ONE THING THAT MADE ME SAD OR MAD TODAY:

_____
_____
_____
_____
_____
_____

ONE THING I LEARNED TODAY:

_____
_____
_____
_____

TODAY'S DATE: _____

TODAY I AM FEELING:

☐ 😊 HAPPY

☐ 😐 JUST OKAY

☐ 😟 SAD

☐ 😠 MAD

ONE WORD I WOULD USE TO DESCRIBE TODAY:

_____

ONE THING THAT MADE ME HAPPY TODAY:

_____
_____
_____
_____
_____
_____
_____

ONE THING THAT MADE ME SAD OR MAD TODAY:

_____
_____
_____
_____
_____
_____

ONE THING I LEARNED TODAY:

_____
_____
_____
_____

TODAY'S DATE: _____

TODAY I AM FEELING:

- ☐ 🙂 HAPPY
- ☐ 😐 JUST OKAY
- ☐ 🙁 SAD
- ☐ ☹️ MAD

ONE WORD I WOULD USE TO DESCRIBE TODAY:

_____

ONE THING THAT MADE ME HAPPY TODAY:

_____
_____
_____
_____
_____
_____
_____

ONE THING THAT MADE ME SAD OR MAD TODAY:

_____
_____
_____
_____
_____
_____
_____

ONE THING I LEARNED TODAY:

_____
_____
_____
_____

TODAY'S DATE: _____

TODAY I AM FEELING:

☐ 😊 HAPPY
☐ 😐 JUST OKAY
☐ ☹️ SAD
☐ 😠 MAD

ONE WORD I WOULD USE TO DESCRIBE TODAY:

_____

ONE THING THAT MADE ME HAPPY TODAY:

_____
_____
_____
_____
_____
_____
_____

ONE THING THAT MADE ME SAD OR MAD TODAY:

_____
_____
_____
_____
_____
_____
_____

ONE THING I LEARNED TODAY:

_____
_____
_____

TODAY'S DATE: _____

TODAY I AM FEELING:

- ☐ 😊 HAPPY
- ☐ 😐 JUST OKAY
- ☐ 😟 SAD
- ☐ 😠 MAD

ONE WORD I WOULD USE TO DESCRIBE TODAY:

_____

ONE THING THAT MADE ME HAPPY TODAY:

_____
_____
_____
_____
_____

ONE THING THAT MADE ME SAD OR MAD TODAY:

_____
_____
_____
_____
_____

ONE THING I LEARNED TODAY:

_____
_____
_____

TODAY'S DATE: _____

TODAY I AM FEELING:

☐ 😊 HAPPY

☐ 😐 JUST OKAY

☐ 😢 SAD

☐ 😠 MAD

ONE WORD I WOULD USE TO DESCRIBE TODAY:
_____

ONE THING THAT MADE ME HAPPY TODAY:
_____
_____
_____
_____
_____
_____
_____

ONE THING THAT MADE ME SAD OR MAD TODAY:
_____
_____
_____
_____
_____
_____
_____

ONE THING I LEARNED TODAY:
_____
_____
_____

TODAY'S DATE: _____

TODAY I AM FEELING:

- [ ] 😊 HAPPY
- [ ] 😐 JUST OKAY
- [ ] 🙁 SAD
- [ ] 😠 MAD

ONE WORD I WOULD USE TO DESCRIBE TODAY:

_____

ONE THING THAT MADE ME HAPPY TODAY:

ONE THING THAT MADE ME SAD OR MAD TODAY:

ONE THING I LEARNED TODAY:

TODAY'S DATE: _____

TODAY I AM FEELING:

- ☐ 🙂 HAPPY
- ☐ 😐 JUST OKAY
- ☐ 🙁 SAD
- ☐ 😠 MAD

ONE WORD I WOULD USE TO DESCRIBE TODAY:

_____

ONE THING THAT MADE ME HAPPY TODAY:

_____

_____

_____

_____

_____

_____

_____

ONE THING THAT MADE ME SAD OR MAD TODAY:

_____

_____

_____

_____

_____

_____

ONE THING I LEARNED TODAY:

_____

_____

_____

TODAY'S DATE: _____

TODAY I AM FEELING:

☐ 🙂 HAPPY
☐ 😐 JUST OKAY
☐ 🙁 SAD
☐ 😠 MAD

ONE WORD I WOULD USE TO DESCRIBE TODAY:

ONE THING THAT MADE ME HAPPY TODAY:

ONE THING THAT MADE ME SAD OR MAD TODAY:

ONE THING I LEARNED TODAY:

TODAY'S DATE: _____

TODAY I AM FEELING:

- ☐ 😊 HAPPY
- ☐ 😐 JUST OKAY
- ☐ 😢 SAD
- ☐ 😠 MAD

ONE WORD I WOULD USE TO DESCRIBE TODAY:

_____

ONE THING THAT MADE ME HAPPY TODAY:

_____
_____
_____
_____
_____
_____
_____
_____

ONE THING THAT MADE ME SAD OR MAD TODAY:

_____
_____
_____
_____
_____
_____
_____

ONE THING I LEARNED TODAY:

_____
_____
_____

TODAY'S DATE: _____

TODAY I AM FEELING:

☐ 😊 HAPPY
☐ 😐 JUST OKAY
☐ 😞 SAD
☐ 😠 MAD

ONE WORD I WOULD USE TO
DESCRIBE TODAY:

_____

ONE THING THAT MADE
ME HAPPY TODAY:

_____
_____
_____
_____
_____
_____

ONE THING THAT MADE
ME SAD OR MAD TODAY:

_____
_____
_____
_____
_____
_____

ONE THING I LEARNED TODAY:

_____
_____
_____
_____

TODAY'S DATE: _____

TODAY I AM FEELING:

- ☐ 🙂 HAPPY
- ☐ 😐 JUST OKAY
- ☐ 🙁 SAD
- ☐ 😠 MAD

ONE WORD I WOULD USE TO DESCRIBE TODAY:

_____

ONE THING THAT MADE ME HAPPY TODAY:

_____
_____
_____
_____
_____
_____
_____

ONE THING THAT MADE ME SAD OR MAD TODAY:

_____
_____
_____
_____
_____
_____
_____

ONE THING I LEARNED TODAY:

_____
_____
_____

TODAY'S DATE: _____

TODAY I AM FEELING:

- ☐ 🙂 HAPPY
- ☐ 😐 JUST OKAY
- ☐ 🙁 SAD
- ☐ 😠 MAD

ONE WORD I WOULD USE TO
DESCRIBE TODAY:

_____

ONE THING THAT MADE
ME HAPPY TODAY:

_____
_____
_____
_____
_____
_____
_____

ONE THING THAT MADE
ME SAD OR MAD TODAY:

_____
_____
_____
_____
_____
_____
_____

ONE THING I LEARNED TODAY:

_____
_____
_____
_____

TODAY'S DATE: _____

TODAY I AM FEELING:

☐ 🙂 HAPPY
☐ 😐 JUST OKAY
☐ 🙁 SAD
☐ 😠 MAD

ONE WORD I WOULD USE TO DESCRIBE TODAY:

_____

ONE THING THAT MADE ME HAPPY TODAY:

_____
_____
_____
_____
_____
_____
_____

ONE THING THAT MADE ME SAD OR MAD TODAY:

_____
_____
_____
_____
_____
_____
_____

ONE THING I LEARNED TODAY:

_____
_____

TODAY'S DATE: _____

TODAY I AM FEELING:

☐ 😊 HAPPY

☐ 😐 JUST OKAY

☐ 🙁 SAD

☐ 😠 MAD

ONE WORD I WOULD USE TO DESCRIBE TODAY:

_____

ONE THING THAT MADE ME HAPPY TODAY:

_____
_____
_____
_____
_____
_____

ONE THING THAT MADE ME SAD OR MAD TODAY:

_____
_____
_____
_____
_____
_____

ONE THING I LEARNED TODAY:

_____
_____
_____

TODAY'S DATE: _____

TODAY I AM FEELING:

☐ 🙂 HAPPY
☐ 😐 JUST OKAY
☐ 🙁 SAD
☐ 😠 MAD

ONE WORD I WOULD USE TO DESCRIBE TODAY:

_____

ONE THING THAT MADE ME HAPPY TODAY:

_____
_____
_____
_____
_____
_____
_____

ONE THING THAT MADE ME SAD OR MAD TODAY:

_____
_____
_____
_____
_____
_____
_____

ONE THING I LEARNED TODAY:

_____
_____
_____
_____

TODAY'S DATE: _____

TODAY I AM FEELING:

- ☐ 🙂 HAPPY
- ☐ 😐 JUST OKAY
- ☐ 🙁 SAD
- ☐ 😠 MAD

ONE WORD I WOULD USE TO DESCRIBE TODAY:

_____

ONE THING THAT MADE ME HAPPY TODAY:

_____
_____
_____
_____
_____
_____
_____

ONE THING THAT MADE ME SAD OR MAD TODAY:

_____
_____
_____
_____
_____
_____
_____

ONE THING I LEARNED TODAY:

_____
_____
_____
_____

TODAY'S DATE: _____

TODAY I AM FEELING:

- ☐ 😊 HAPPY
- ☐ 😐 JUST OKAY
- ☐ 🙁 SAD
- ☐ 😠 MAD

ONE WORD I WOULD USE TO DESCRIBE TODAY:

_____

ONE THING THAT MADE ME HAPPY TODAY:

_____
_____
_____
_____
_____
_____
_____
_____

ONE THING THAT MADE ME SAD OR MAD TODAY:

_____
_____
_____
_____
_____
_____
_____

ONE THING I LEARNED TODAY:

_____
_____
_____

TODAY'S DATE: _____

TODAY I AM FEELING:

- [ ] 😊 HAPPY
- [ ] 😐 JUST OKAY
- [ ] 😢 SAD
- [ ] 😠 MAD

ONE WORD I WOULD USE TO DESCRIBE TODAY:

_____

ONE THING THAT MADE ME HAPPY TODAY:

_____
_____
_____
_____
_____
_____
_____

ONE THING THAT MADE ME SAD OR MAD TODAY:

_____
_____
_____
_____
_____
_____
_____

ONE THING I LEARNED TODAY:

_____
_____
_____
_____

TODAY'S DATE: _____

TODAY I AM FEELING:

☐ 😊 HAPPY

☐ 😐 JUST OKAY

☐ 🙁 SAD

☐ 😠 MAD

ONE WORD I WOULD USE TO DESCRIBE TODAY:

_____

ONE THING THAT MADE ME HAPPY TODAY:

_____
_____
_____
_____
_____
_____
_____

ONE THING THAT MADE ME SAD OR MAD TODAY:

_____
_____
_____
_____
_____
_____
_____

ONE THING I LEARNED TODAY:

_____
_____
_____

TODAY'S DATE: _____

TODAY I AM FEELING:

- ☐ 🙂 HAPPY
- ☐ 😐 JUST OKAY
- ☐ 🙁 SAD
- ☐ 😣 MAD

ONE WORD I WOULD USE TO DESCRIBE TODAY:
_____

ONE THING THAT MADE ME HAPPY TODAY:
_____
_____
_____
_____
_____

ONE THING THAT MADE ME SAD OR MAD TODAY:
_____
_____
_____
_____
_____

ONE THING I LEARNED TODAY:
_____
_____
_____
_____

TODAY'S DATE: _____

TODAY I AM FEELING:

- ☐ 😊 HAPPY
- ☐ 😐 JUST OKAY
- ☐ 😟 SAD
- ☐ 😠 MAD

ONE WORD I WOULD USE TO DESCRIBE TODAY:

_____

ONE THING THAT MADE ME HAPPY TODAY:

ONE THING THAT MADE ME SAD OR MAD TODAY:

ONE THING I LEARNED TODAY:

TODAY'S DATE: _____

TODAY I AM FEELING:

- [ ] 🙂 HAPPY
- [ ] 😐 JUST OKAY
- [ ] ☹️ SAD
- [ ] 😠 MAD

ONE WORD I WOULD USE TO DESCRIBE TODAY:

_____

ONE THING THAT MADE ME HAPPY TODAY:

_____
_____
_____
_____
_____
_____

ONE THING THAT MADE ME SAD OR MAD TODAY:

_____
_____
_____
_____
_____
_____

ONE THING I LEARNED TODAY:

_____
_____
_____

TODAY'S DATE: _____

TODAY I AM FEELING:

☐ 😊 HAPPY
☐ 😐 JUST OKAY
☐ 🙁 SAD
☐ ☹️ MAD

ONE WORD I WOULD USE TO
DESCRIBE TODAY:

_____

ONE THING THAT MADE
ME HAPPY TODAY:

_____
_____
_____
_____
_____
_____
_____

ONE THING THAT MADE
ME SAD OR MAD TODAY:

_____
_____
_____
_____
_____
_____
_____

ONE THING I LEARNED TODAY:

_____
_____
_____

TODAY'S DATE: _____

TODAY I AM FEELING:

☐ 🙂 HAPPY
☐ 😐 JUST OKAY
☐ 🙁 SAD
☐ 😠 MAD

ONE WORD I WOULD USE TO DESCRIBE TODAY:

_____

ONE THING THAT MADE ME HAPPY TODAY:

_____
_____
_____
_____
_____
_____
_____

ONE THING THAT MADE ME SAD OR MAD TODAY:

_____
_____
_____
_____
_____
_____
_____

ONE THING I LEARNED TODAY:

_____
_____
_____

TODAY'S DATE: _____

TODAY I AM FEELING:

- [ ] 😊 HAPPY
- [ ] 😐 JUST OKAY
- [ ] 🙁 SAD
- [ ] 😠 MAD

ONE WORD I WOULD USE TO DESCRIBE TODAY:

_____

ONE THING THAT MADE ME HAPPY TODAY:

_____
_____
_____
_____
_____
_____
_____

ONE THING THAT MADE ME SAD OR MAD TODAY:

_____
_____
_____
_____
_____
_____
_____

ONE THING I LEARNED TODAY:

_____
_____
_____

TODAY'S DATE: _____

TODAY I AM FEELING:

- ☐ 😊 HAPPY
- ☐ 😐 JUST OKAY
- ☐ 🙁 SAD
- ☐ 😠 MAD

ONE WORD I WOULD USE TO DESCRIBE TODAY:

_____

ONE THING THAT MADE ME HAPPY TODAY:

_____
_____
_____
_____
_____
_____
_____

ONE THING THAT MADE ME SAD OR MAD TODAY:

_____
_____
_____
_____
_____
_____
_____

ONE THING I LEARNED TODAY:

_____
_____
_____
_____

TODAY'S DATE: _____

TODAY I AM FEELING:

☐ 😊 HAPPY

☐ 😐 JUST OKAY

☐ 🙁 SAD

☐ 😠 MAD

ONE WORD I WOULD USE TO DESCRIBE TODAY:

_____

ONE THING THAT MADE ME HAPPY TODAY:

_____
_____
_____
_____
_____
_____
_____

ONE THING THAT MADE ME SAD OR MAD TODAY:

_____
_____
_____
_____
_____
_____

ONE THING I LEARNED TODAY:

_____
_____
_____

TODAY'S DATE: _____

TODAY I AM FEELING:

☐ 😊 HAPPY
☐ 😐 JUST OKAY
☐ 😞 SAD
☐ 😠 MAD

ONE WORD I WOULD USE TO DESCRIBE TODAY:

_____

ONE THING THAT MADE ME HAPPY TODAY:

_____
_____
_____
_____
_____
_____

ONE THING THAT MADE ME SAD OR MAD TODAY:

_____
_____
_____
_____
_____
_____

ONE THING I LEARNED TODAY:

_____
_____
_____
_____

TODAY'S DATE: _____

TODAY I AM FEELING:

☐ 😊 HAPPY

☐ 😐 JUST OKAY

☐ 🙁 SAD

☐ 😠 MAD

ONE WORD I WOULD USE TO DESCRIBE TODAY:

_____

ONE THING THAT MADE ME HAPPY TODAY:

_____
_____
_____
_____
_____
_____
_____

ONE THING THAT MADE ME SAD OR MAD TODAY:

_____
_____
_____
_____
_____
_____
_____

ONE THING I LEARNED TODAY:

_____
_____
_____

TODAY'S DATE: _____

TODAY I AM FEELING:

- ☐ 🙂 HAPPY
- ☐ 😐 JUST OKAY
- ☐ 🙁 SAD
- ☐ ☹️ MAD

ONE WORD I WOULD USE TO DESCRIBE TODAY:

_____

ONE THING THAT MADE ME HAPPY TODAY:

_____
_____
_____
_____
_____
_____
_____
_____

ONE THING THAT MADE ME SAD OR MAD TODAY:

_____
_____
_____
_____
_____
_____
_____
_____

ONE THING I LEARNED TODAY:

_____
_____
_____
_____

TODAY'S DATE: _____

TODAY I AM FEELING:

☐ 😊 HAPPY

☐ 😐 JUST OKAY

☐ ☹ SAD

☐ 😠 MAD

ONE WORD I WOULD USE TO
DESCRIBE TODAY:

_____

ONE THING THAT MADE
ME HAPPY TODAY:

_____
_____
_____
_____
_____
_____
_____
_____

ONE THING THAT MADE
ME SAD OR MAD TODAY:

_____
_____
_____
_____
_____
_____
_____

ONE THING I LEARNED TODAY:

_____
_____
_____

Made in the USA
Columbia, SC
05 October 2023

23943254R00057